AN INSIDE LOOK AT THE
U.S. NAVY
SEALs

JOE FUNK

ISBN 978-0-545-42289-5

10 9 8 7 6 5 4 3 2 1   11 12 13 14 15

Printed in the U.S.A.   40

First edition, September 2011

Created and designed by Mojo Media Inc.: Author/Editor, Joe Funk; Art Director, Daniel Tideman; Assistant Editor, Rob Jaskula

All photos courtesy of the U.S. Navy SEALs except as follows. Page 14 bottom: AP Photo/Elise Amendola; pages 16–17: AP Photo/ Pier Paolo Cito; page 19: AP Photo/Haraz N. Ghanbari; page 22: Dreamstime; page 27 inset: AP Photo/Ed Andrieski; page 31 inset: AP Photo/Ahn Young-joon; pages 34–35 background and inset: AP Photo/James R. Evans/U.S. Navy/dapd; page 37: AP Photo/Robyn Gerstenslager/U.S. Navy; pages 38–39 background: Daniel Blatter/UPI/Newscom; page 38 inset: Reuters/Ho New; page 39 inset: AP Photo/Win McNamee; page 40: Reuters/Ho New; page 41: Robert J. Fluegel/AFP/Getty Images/Newscom; page 42: AP Photo/ Jacquelyn Martin; page 43: AP Photo/The White House, Pete Souza; page 44: AP Photo/Rex Features; page 45: AP Photo/Aqeel Ahmed.

CONTENTS

WHAT IS A SEAL?

The **United States Navy SEALs** are among the most elite fighting forces in the world. Trained to operate in the **SE**a, **A**ir, and **L**and (which creates the acronym for their name), their small teams are sent on some of the hardest missions the United States conducts, all in the interest of protecting our country. Often operating in the most dangerous hot spots around the globe, SEALs work silently and stealthily, and can carry out their missions any time of day or night.

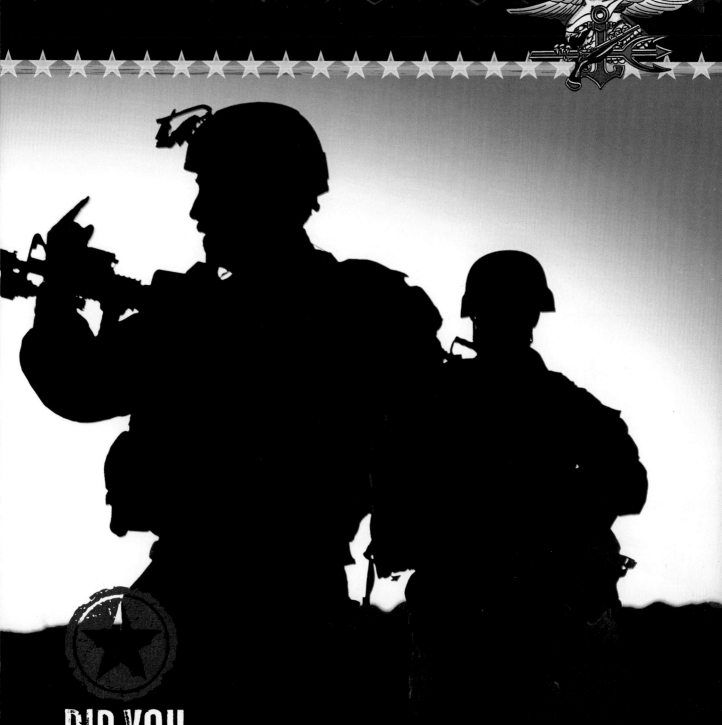

DID YOU KNOW?

The legendary Navy SEALs are usually anonymous and operate in secret, but they make up one of the greatest fighting forces the world has ever seen. A quiet group of professionals, SEALs eagerly train for their missions and serve with great pride, even if their exploits are never revealed in detail.

U.S. NAVY SEALs

★★★★★★★★★★★★★★★★★★★★★★★★

SEALs come from the United States Navy, and occasionally the Coast Guard, and are put through one of the toughest physical courses ever created to earn their Special Warfare insignia, known as a Trident. Their training focuses on developing each SEAL as a virtual one-man army who can also work well with a team to accomplish mission goals.

As part of the Naval Special Warfare Command, SEALs have been called the "tip of the spear" because they are elite members of our nation's forces—the best of the best. President John F. Kennedy established the first two SEAL teams in January 1962. These initial SEAL teams were descendents of covert units and underwater demolition teams that had served in previous wars.

The navy's underwater demolition teams were the forerunners of the Navy SEALs.

The SEALs' original mission was to conduct secret underwater operations in seas and rivers, and they were initially utilized in the Vietnam War. Their first operation was actually a training mission— they taught the South Vietnamese how to conduct amphibious military maneuvers.

President Kennedy authorized the funding to enhance the special operations arms of the military in the same speech that announced the government's plan to put a man on the moon. The navy determined that its role in the expanded special forces should focus on counter-guerilla operations.

TRAINING REQUIREMENTS

Training to become an actively deployed SEAL is one of the toughest tasks in our military. Successfully completing the courses necessary to become a SEAL is the mark of the truly elite.

All SEALs must be men from the navy or coast guard who are by nature smart, fit, and mentally tough. To be considered for training, potential candidates must pass comprehensive written and physical exams, including a 500-yard swim and a 1.5-mile run. Their emotional fortitude is analyzed in three categories: performance strategies, psychological resilience, and personality traits.

Throughout the rigors of training to be SEALs, candidates must work together through hardship to accomplish goals as a team.

Prospective SEALs are then judged on their total results, with each case handled individually. They must score well on both exams, and although they may repeat the elements of the physical test, the mental exam score is permanent and the test cannot be retaken.

Once accepted, prospective SEALs enter one of the most rigorous training programs in the world. They begin with two months in the northern suburbs of Chicago on Lake Michigan, working to improve their physical fitness before the rest of training. If they make it through one final physical test, they move on to southern California for a three-week introduction to the demanding training of a SEAL.

The next seven weeks are some of the toughest, designed to build physical fitness and mental resilience. In one period of five and a half days, candidates run more than two hundred miles and are permitted only about four hours of sleep the entire time. The next two phases focus on underwater fighting and the land warfare skills the SEALs need for their operations. After qualification training, which prepares them for the types of operations they'll face in the field, candidates finally become SEALs.

Training to become a SEAL is a mixture of learning tactical knowledge for operating in the field and hard physical training. To excel, SEALs must be trained to be the very best, and that includes pushing their bodies to the max.

EVERYDAY
ROUTINE & DIET

It takes over thirty months for a SEAL to finish his training and be ready for his first deployment. Though the formal schooling is over, the education never ceases. SEALs are constantly honing new skills in classrooms and in the field, both tactics for their specific jobs and unit training for team-building purposes. The emphasis on fitness is relentless: SEALs are among the fittest members of the U.S. military, so running, swimming, and other cross-training exercises remain a top priority.

A SEAL brushes sand off his shoulders after finishing a training exercise. Even after a candidate becomes a SEAL, the training doesn't end—SEALs must constantly work to maintain their fitness and skills.

DID YOU KNOW?

SEALs must train at all times for the different environments they might face. Being a SEAL is a lifestyle that involves a full commitment—they can be training one day and find themselves deep into a mission the next. One unique factor is that when they are deployed, a strong web of secrecy surrounds SEALs: They ordinarily cannot reveal any details about where they are, including the weather or time of day.

Navy SEALs are on location in about thirty different countries at any given time, allowing them to get anywhere quickly and execute missions at a moment's notice. Because of the nature of their work, SEALs can never anticipate what the next mission might bring.

Navy SEAL teams are based in one of three locations: Coronado, California; Little Creek, Virginia; and Pearl Harbor, Hawaii. The California station houses the command center of the SEALs as well as their training program. SEAL Teams One, Three, Five, and Seven are based there. The Virginia location is home to SEAL Teams Two, Four, Eight, and Ten, as well as a reserve unit. The Hawaii station houses a special vehicle delivery team.

Because they expend so much energy training, keeping fit, and executing their missions, SEALs must be well nourished. It takes a lot of calories to fuel up a Navy SEAL, given the hard workload. While on base, SEALs eat typical mess hall fare, with extra carbohydrates for more energy. The focus is on keeping their lean, muscular bodies energized and limber so they can perform the many difficult maneuvers required of them.

SEALs burn an extraordinary amount of calories—whether performing underwater missions, jumping out of aircraft, or just maintaining their peak fitness levels—so a well-balanced diet is a must.

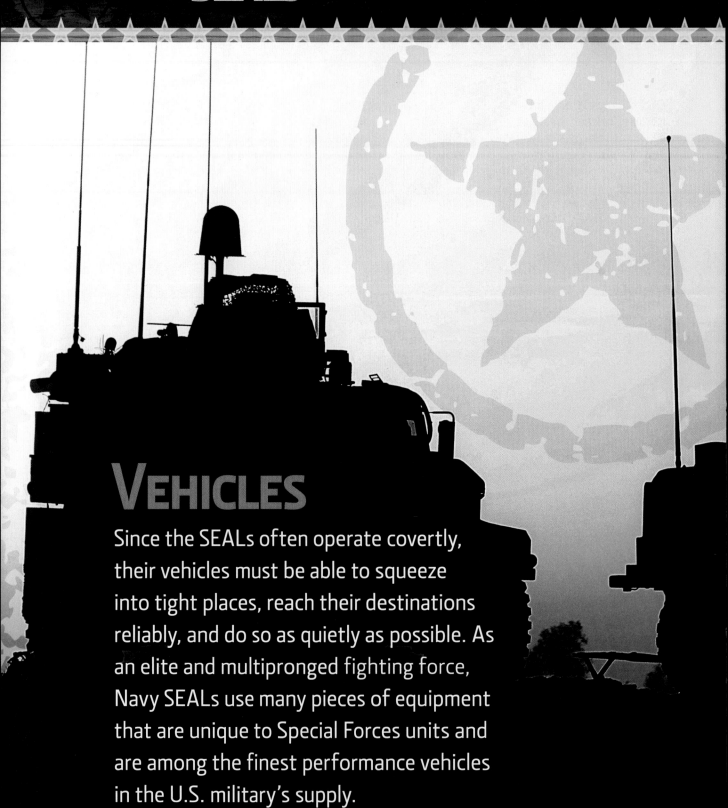

VEHICLES

Since the SEALs often operate covertly, their vehicles must be able to squeeze into tight places, reach their destinations reliably, and do so as quietly as possible. As an elite and multipronged fighting force, Navy SEALs use many pieces of equipment that are unique to Special Forces units and are among the finest performance vehicles in the U.S. military's supply.

DID YOU KNOW?

Though it may look haphazard, the placement of antennas on an MRAP (the SEALs' land vehicle of choice) is the product of much study. Antennas serve communications and electronic

U.S. NAVY SEALs

★ ★ ★ ★ ★ ★ ★ ★ ★ ★ ★ ★ ★ ★ ★ ★ ★ ★

Carrying up to four Navy SEALs, the Desert Patrol Vehicle (DPV) is one of the most versatile vehicles in the U.S. military. Though it resembles a go-cart, there's nothing childish about the DPV. Powered by a perky engine, the DPV can get into rough areas quickly and navigate just about any terrain. Its small size can also make deployment easier.

Whether in the deserts of Iraq or in the mountains of Afghanistan, SEALs need a reliable vehicle for getting around and staying safe. An outgrowth of the popular High Mobility Multipurpose Wheeled Vehicle (HMMWV), the Ground Mobility Vehicle (GMV) is a workhorse for SEALs on the ground. With many features different from those on the original HMMWV, GMVs can more easily be adapted for specific missions.

The MRAP was designed to be a safer armored fighting vehicle for our troops. Thanks to the shape of its hull, it is better able to resist roadside explosives, including IEDs.

A new kind of armored fighting vehicle, dubbed Mine Resistant Ambush Protected (MRAP), is a unique military project—there are several different designs that see active service. This makes MRAPs adaptable to the needs of whatever unit employs them. MRAPs feature the latest antimine technology to keep the fighting men inside safer than they would be in a standard HMMWV. The SEALs began using them in 2008, and they are rapidly seeing more widespread use.

The current standard military rifle, the M4 carbine sees use throughout the armed services. Its compact size and short barrel make it easy to carry into any situation, and the array of accessories that it can accommodate allow it to adapt to any mission.

WEAPONS

Navy SEALs have the ability to adapt their equipment to whatever suits their needs. If they need specific tools to accomplish a mission, they can easily acquire them. Because of this, there is no universal field outfitting for SEALs. Their weapons include some of the most common military weapons as well as several used only by the SEALs.

DID YOU KNOW?

In its standard issue, the M4A1 features a 14.5-inch barrel, making it maneuverable in tight spaces. Some of the many accessories that can be fitted to the M4A1 are night-vision devices, grenade launchers, suppressors, and upgraded sights. Militaries and police forces from over forty countries around the world use the M4 and its variants.

Many SEALs use the M4A1 carbine, the most common firearm among U.S. ground-fighting special forces. However, the SEALs usually use a unique firearm called the Close Quarters Battle Receiver. This weapon allows SEALs to operate in tight areas, including in rooms in houses: Its barrel is shorter than that of a standard M4, and it also allows room for a suppressor to be fitted for close combat, making the SEALs stealthier.

One of the weapons used by the Navy SEALs in Iraq just celebrated its fiftieth birthday. The M79 grenade launcher still sees active service, even though other branches of the military largely replaced it before the end of the Vietnam War. Though they relegate it mainly to an antimine role, the SEALs make the reliable and battle-tested M79 one of the oldest weapons still in service.

Considered among the best shots in the world, Navy SEAL snipers can eliminate targets from a range that may reach up to a mile. Able to take out high-profile targets in enemy-held areas or pirates located on bobbing ships across a stretch of open ocean, these sharpshooters have cool nerves and steady hands. Snipers tailor their weapons to the specific situations they will be in, and they can select from more than half a dozen different high-performance, large-caliber rifles.

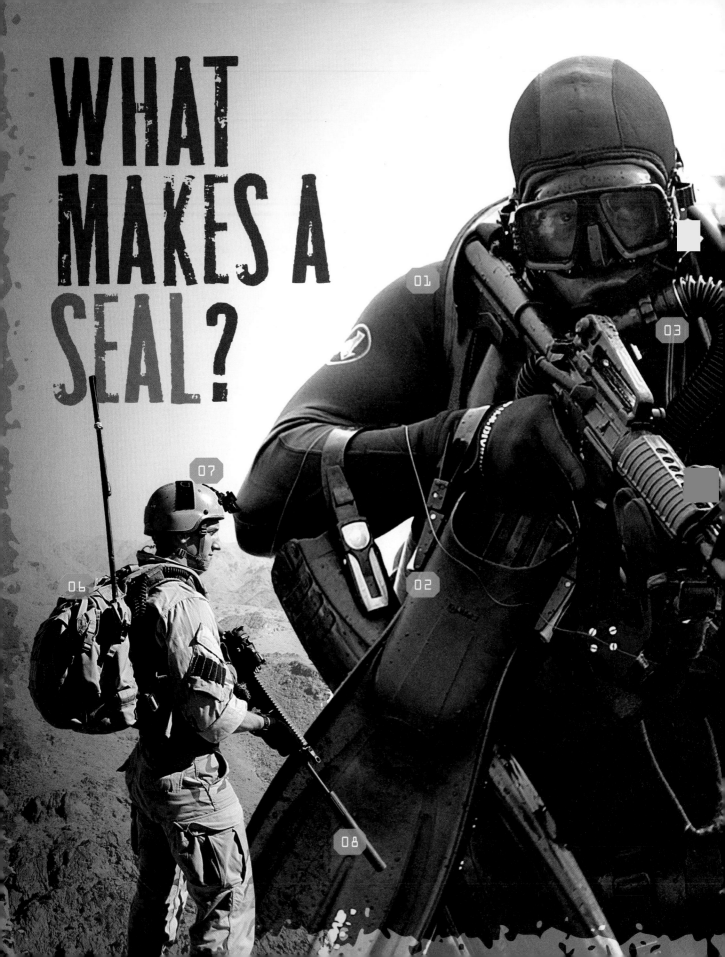

WHAT MAKES A SEAL?

01

03

07

06

02

08

04

05

09

10

GADGETS

Due to the dangerous nature of their operations, SEALs rely on the latest technology to help them stay undetected and accomplish their missions. The gadgets they use may seem straight out of an action movie, but in reality they are highly specialized tools used in unique, ingenious, and devastatingly effective ways. Though many of the gadgets outfitted to SEALs were originally intended to be classified, some have proven so successful, they are now being adopted by other branches of the military and even by civilians.

GPS technology can fit in the palm of a hand and is a common sight today, but its original uses were military in nature. The network of satellites is still maintained by the Department of Defense.

Infrared cameras and night-vision goggles are virtually essential for SEALs. With these, SEALs are able to detect threats and enemies in the dark—vital for the night operations that they are so commonly a part of. Tiny, helmet-mounted cameras can also link back to headquarters, allowing commanders to see what the SEALs see. During the operation against Osama bin Laden, President Barack Obama and his aides in the Situation Room at the White House were apparently able to see and hear parts of the mission unfold in real time, thanks to the cameras.

An older SEAL technology is now in widespread use among the civilian population: GPS. Able to pinpoint locations more precisely than maps (though SEALs carry those, too), handheld Global Positioning System units help keep SEALs from straying off course and enable SEAL snipers to locate their targets as accurately as possible. The Defense Advanced GPS Receiver is the current GPS unit in active service, and it provides several capabilities not found in civilian GPS units, such as the ability to break through enemy attempts to jam its signal.

Because they work quietly and often at night, the Navy SEALs rely on night-vision technology to see what's ahead of them. Additionally, advanced optic systems used with their weapons help SEALs identify targets while in the midst of combat.

WATERCRAFT

Since the Navy SEALs are an amphibious force, they are often deployed into hostile areas in or under the water. As their missions are incredibly varied, they rely on a number of fascinating watercraft to place them in key hot spots, then extract them after their missions are complete. Though they use other navy ships for long-range transportation, SEALs rely on some small and unique vessels when the time comes for action.

Since SEALs can trace their history back to underwater combat units, it's no surprise that they often carry out their missions at least partially underwater. To deliver a SEAL team without a boat on the surface, a SEAL Delivery Vehicle is often used. This minisubmersible ferries SEALs as well as their pilots very quietly underwater. Since it is not enclosed, it can be modified with its own oxygen supplies to carry SEALs over longer distances.

Because SEALs rely on elements of stealth and surprise, Combat Rubber Raiding Craft are a mainstay of operations when SEALs make an amphibious landing. Resembling rubber boats, and often mistaken for run-of-the-mill inflatable dinghies, these special watercraft are designed to be as inconspicuous as possible, to avoid detection. They are much tougher than they look and are able to navigate some very rough seas while also being lightweight, compact, and easy to inflate.

Another unique way SEALs are inserted into an area is from a specially modified nuclear submarine that carries a Dry Deck Shelter, an attachment that allows divers to slip into the water while the submarine is submerged. Each Dry Deck Shelter can place a SEAL Delivery Vehicle or four Combat Rubber Raiding Craft with twenty SEALs into a hostile area without requiring the submarine to surface.

DID YOU KNOW?

The SEAL Delivery Vehicle is powered by batteries and features navigation, communication, and life-support systems for the SEALs on board. Its supply of compressed air helps extend the range of the air tank, or rebreather, each SEAL on board is wearing.

The C-130 has been a part of the U.S. military for over fifty years. With over forty models and types, the Hercules has taken part in countless operations all over the world.

AIRCRAFT

The SEALs aren't only a water and land fighting force; they are also often flown into or out of their missions, making them even more effective. Because of the secret nature of their missions, their aircraft must be hard to detect, and as versatile as the warriors they carry. The SEALs have just about all aircraft in the U.S. military at their disposal, and they tailor their selections to specific missions.

★ ★ ★ ★ ★ ★ ★ ★ ★ ★ ★ ★ ★ ★ ★ ★ ★ ★

Able to operate from almost any runway surface, the C-130 Hercules is the primary transport aircraft of today's military. With over fifty years of service, the C-130 is one of the longest-serving military planes in history. It is used by the SEALs for parachuting men (sometimes with dogs) and their equipment into mission areas. Thanks to its high cargo capacity, it can even drop SEAL vehicles with the men.

The SEAL team that raided the bin Laden compound in Pakistan flew in another of the military's iconic aircraft, the Black Hawk helicopter. Since its introduction in 1979, the twin-engine chopper has seen action in every major military theater the United States has engaged in. The latest version used by the SEALs has a modified tail section and utilizes stealth technology to help make it less visible to enemy radar.

SEALs make use of intelligence gathered by the air force and the CIA from unmanned aerial vehicles like the MQ-1 Predator drone. Able to get up-close intelligence on a target area and relay real-time information without putting lives at risk, the Predator has become a vital part of the eyes and ears of the U.S. military. Many of its capabilities are still classified.

DID YOU KNOW?

One of the greatest helicopter designs of all time, the CH-47 Chinook has seen active service since 1962. It's of great value to the SEALs thanks to its versatility and its ability to deal with all sorts of temperatures and altitudes. The version used by the Special Forces features a larger fuel capacity, and ground-following radar.

DOGS

A dog is a human's best friend and can also be a super sidekick for a soldier. Dogs have been fighting alongside American forces since the Civil War and were officially inducted into the military as army dogs during World War II. Today there are more than three thousand dogs in the U.S. military, with mostly German shepherds and Belgian Malinois serving beside the Navy SEALs. Navy SEAL dogs can be trained for all kinds of tasks, including tracking targets, sniffing for explosives, and attacking enemies.

A vital part of a military working dog's skill set is its natural ability to see in less light. The dogs can venture into areas that are too dark for humans to see in and, thanks to infrared cameras, can relay information about what lies ahead to the SEALs they work with.

Defense Secretary Robert Gates greets one of America's canine combatants, a bomb-sniffing dog named Rinus—along with his handler, Sergeant Guillermo Castellanos—in Kandahar, Afghanistan, in late 2010.

U.S. NAVY SEALs

These animals are much more effective in certain roles than humans or machines are. For instance, their ability to sniff out explosives far exceeds any robotic technology the U.S. military has come up with. They can also detect booby traps and even people, alerting their soldier handlers to threats that might not otherwise have been discovered. The Navy SEALs deployed to capture or kill Osama bin Laden were joined by one heroic dog, a Belgian Malinois named Cairo, on their mission.

If targets attempt to flee, the dogs can be vital in preventing their escape. They can run twice as fast as humans and have extremely powerful jaws. The dogs are trained to bite and hold on, which makes for a practical way to intimidate or apprehend suspects without shooting at them.

The SEALs sometimes suit their dogs with tactical vests when the dogs are scouting. The vests cost more than twenty thousand dollars each but serve an important purpose. Because the suits are equipped with infrared and night-vision cameras, handlers can use monitors nearly a mile away to see what the dogs can see—an invaluable tool for scanning an area before sending SEALs in.

It's not a bad idea to keep military working dogs muzzled. Their bite is one of their most important weapons, as it can really stop a fleeing enemy. With its sharp teeth, a dog can bite with hundreds of pounds of force.

A jet airliner is lined up to hit one of the World Trade Center towers in New York City on Sept. 11, 2001. Osama bin Laden (right, in 1998 photo) was killed by a special operation in Pakistan. AP FILE PHOTOS

ARIZONA REPUBLIC
A GANNETT COMPANY

U.S. KILLS BIN LADEN

al-Qaida leader killed in raid in Pakistan

body is in custody of U.S. forces

THE BIN LADEN OPERATION

After over a decade of hiding, Osama bin Laden—the mastermind behind multiple attacks on the United States and other countries—met his doom at the hands of the U.S. Navy SEALs. The Naval Special Warfare Development Group, the former SEAL Team Six, was tasked by President Obama to conduct Operation Neptune Spear in Pakistan on May 2, 2011, to take down bin Laden by any means necessary.

Surrounded by military leaders and government officials, President Obama watched the entire bin Laden operation from the White House's Situation Room.

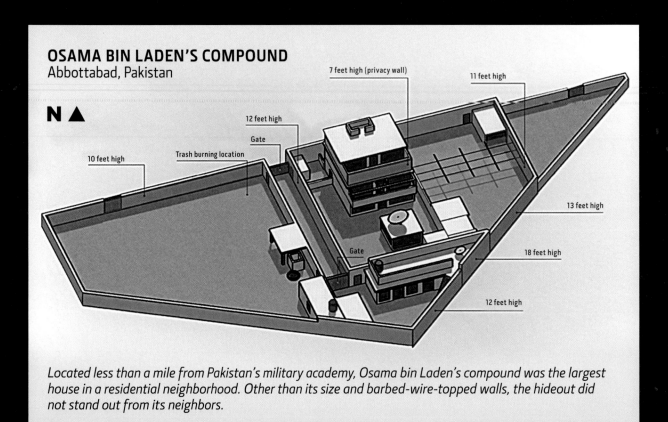

OSAMA BIN LADEN'S COMPOUND
Abbottabad, Pakistan

N ▲

7 feet high (privacy wall)
11 feet high
12 feet high
Gate
Trash burning location
10 feet high
13 feet high
Gate
18 feet high
12 feet high

Located less than a mile from Pakistan's military academy, Osama bin Laden's compound was the largest house in a residential neighborhood. Other than its size and barbed-wire-topped walls, the hideout did not stand out from its neighbors.

Through intelligence gathered from captured members of al-Qaeda, the United States was able to learn that one of bin Laden's most trusted messengers had a curious-looking home in Pakistan. After surveying the area over a period of several years, the government figured out that a high-profile terrorist was housed there, perhaps bin Laden himself. President Obama gave the go-ahead for the mission, selecting the SEALs for one of the most important U.S. military operations in recent history.

The Navy SEALs who carried out the mission were transported by stealth Black Hawk helicopters flown from a base in Afghanistan. They were equipped with M4 carbines, sidearms, and night-vision goggles. Because they were operating covertly, the helicopters swooped in very low to avoid detection systems, hugging the terrain. Despite a mechanical problem with one of the helicopters, which prevented the SEALs from landing inside the compound, they began their mission just after one A.M. local time, on a

After the raid, local Pakistanis milled outside the residence and were apparently stunned to learn that the most wanted man in the world was living in their neighborhood for years.

moonless night. They landed outside the compound and quickly blew a hole in the structure's outer wall.

The SEALs encountered limited resistance and quickly dispatched their enemies as they raced their way from the ground up through the three-story complex. Bin Laden's presence was confirmed for the first time when he leaned out of a third-floor window. Moments later, the SEALs then finally dispatched the man who had evaded the United States and its allies for more than a decade. The brave SEALs had been in the compound from entry to exit for less than forty minutes and had accomplished the goals of their raid. A helicopter whisked them off to an air base, and into legend.

TERMINOLOGY

Cross training—Combining different types of maneuvers and combat programs to maximize the benefits of all. A distinct feature of the Special Forces, military cross training allows soldiers to learn multiple specialties so they can be applied in any situation.

Deployment—Moving from one area to another destination, often to combat zones. Not only men but also their vehicles and other materials must be moved. Deployments can be brief or may last for over a year.

Hot spot—An area where intense conflict is taking place. When a hot spot requires rapid intervention, Special Forces like the Navy SEALs are often called upon to deal with threats quickly and covertly.

Military working dog—A dog that is trained by the military to complete a number of tasks. Dogs have been a part of warfare since ancient times and remain important today. Used to track enemies, detect mines, scout enemy-held ground, and guard camps or bases, military working dogs serve in roles not well suited for humans.

Radar—The most common type of object detection. Radar uses radio waves to determine the location of objects. It can determine the range, altitude, speed, and direction of many objects, including aircraft, ships, missiles, and vehicles. This is done by transmitting waves that bounce off the objects, returning the signal back to an antenna.

SEAL candidate—A man undergoing training to become a Navy SEAL. Typically sailors at the beginning of their naval careers, SEAL candidates undergo some of the most rigorous training in the world.

Suppressor—A device attached to the end of the barrel of a gun that quiets the noise and helps minimize the flash of the weapon. Since SEALs are often operating covertly, it is imperative to make as little commotion as possible.

Training regimen—A structured program that prepares a Navy SEAL mentally and physically to perform specialized activities and maintain optimum general fitness.

Earn Your Trident Everyday

U.S. NAVY SEAL CODE

★ Loyalty to Country, Team, and Teammate

★ Serve with Honor and Integrity On and Off the Battlefield

★ Ready to Lead, Ready to Follow, Never Quit

★ Take Responsibility for your Actions and the Actions of your Teammates

★ Excel as Warriors through Discipline and Innovation

★ Train for War, Fight to Win, Defeat our Nation's Enemies